# Crucial Conversations ...in 30 minutes

THE EXPERT GUIDE TO **KERRY PATTERSON,
JOSEPH GRENNY, RON MCMILLAN, AND AL SWITZLER'S**

# Crucial
# Conversations
## ...in 30 minutes

**THE 30 MINUTE EXPERT SERIES**

**GARAMOND**
— PRESS —

**A NOTE TO THE READER: You should purchase and read the book that has been reviewed. This book is meant to accompany a reading of the reviewed book and is neither intended nor offered as a substitute for the reviewed book.**

**This review is unofficial and unauthorized. This book is not authorized, approved, licensed, or endorsed by Kerry Patterson, Joseph Grenny, Ron McMillan, Al Switzler or McGraw-Hill.**

ISBN: 978-1-62315-179-9 Print | 978-1-62315-180-5 eBook

# Contents

# At a Glance

This book is an extended review of *Crucial Conversations: Tools for Talking When Stakes Are High*, published by McGraw-Hill. In this best seller, authors Kerry Patterson, Joseph Grenny, Ron McMillan, and Al Switzler explain how to create meaningful dialogue that leads to productive outcomes. With years of research and thousands of testimonials, the authors explain how to develop mutual purpose and respect, create an atmosphere of safety, and explore motivations to teach you to have conversations that will improve business, relationships, and personal health.

This review begins with a brief presentation of the book and its authors. You'll learn about the inspiration for *Crucial Conversations*, and you'll come away with an initial impression of how readers have responded to the book. You'll also meet the authors and learn a few things about their lives and work.

Next comes a short digest of readers' responses to the book—the good and the not so good, from mainstream book reviewers to bloggers and other interested readers.

The following two sections of the review offer a synopsis of the book and a detailed discussion of its key concepts. Here, you'll find examples of the key concepts in practice and ideas for applying them to your own life and experience.

Finally, the main points of this review are briefly restated, in a way that may well leave you eager to get your own copy of the book and see for yourself what the buzz is all about. Also included is a list of important terms used in *Crucial Conversations* and recommendations for further reading about how to create powerful, nonthreatening, and persuasive dialogue that will improve the quality of your professional and personal life.

# Understanding
# *Crucial Conversations*

## ABOUT THE BOOK

When the authors first began their work together, they were interested more in crucial moments than in crucial conversations. They wanted to identify the key instances when people's behaviors and actions dramatically affected their personal and professional lives. By observing top performers, they learned that most life-changing moments occur around emotionally and politically risky interactions; thus, an individual's success depends on their ability to handle crucial conversations, when emotions are charged and stakes are high. With this discovery, the authors created *Crucial Conversations,* a book to teach people the skills they need to handle difficult conversations successfully and achieve maximum results.

First published in 2002, *Crucial Conversations* has sold more than two million copies and was on the best-seller lists of the *New York Times, BusinessWeek,* the *Washington Post,* and the *Wall Street Journal.* With additional research and thousands of success stories to guide them, the second edition was published in 2011, featuring readers' stories, links to videos, and summaries of new findings. The book has been translated into many languages, including Hebrew and Arabic, and has been used to create meaningful discourse in areas of conflict, such as Kabul and Cairo, as well as areas of prosperity and growth, such as Boston and Bangkok. According to the VitalSmarts team, the corporate training group founded by the authors, three hundred of the companies in the Fortune 500 have used the skills taught in *Crucial Conversations* to master delicate situations and achieve further success.

## ABOUT THE AUTHORS

*Crucial Conversations* is the result of a collaboration of expertise. In addition to this book, Kerry Patterson, Joseph Grenny, Ron McMillan, and Al Switzler have written three other *New York Times* best sellers: *Crucial Confrontations: Tools for Resolving Broken Promises, Violated Expectations, and Bad Behavior*; *Influencer: The Power to Change Anything*; and *Change Anything: The New Science of Personal Success*. In 2007 the authors were named Ernst & Young Entrepreneurs Of The Year for their work with Vital-Smarts, the company they cofounded in 1990 to provide corporate training and promote sustained and measurable changes in behavior. Named the 2008 Business of the Year by the Association of Learning Providers, Vital-Smarts was recognized by *Inc.* magazine as one of the fastest-growing companies in America. Here's a bit more about each of the authors' individual accomplishments.

- Kerry Patterson received his doctorate from Stanford University. He cofounded Interact Performance Systems, and for ten years served as its vice president of research and development. He has taught at Brigham Young University's Marriott School of Management, where he received a Mentor of the Year Award and the William G. Dyer Distinguished Alumni Award for his contributions in organizational behavior.

- Joseph Grenny is cofounder of California Computer Corporation. For the past thirty years, he has consulted on corporate change initiatives, meeting with leaders and executives worldwide. He has appeared on more than a hundred radio and television programs, and he writes a column on leadership for *BusinessWeek*.

- Ron McMillan is an expert on influence and leadership, and he is highly sought after as a speaker by top-tier companies such as Disney, AT&T, and Nike. He is cofounder of the Covey Leadership Center.

- Al Switzler is the former president of two consulting firms and is currently the director of training and management development at a large health care organization. He is a frequent keynote speaker at leading companies such as Lockheed Martin, Ford, and IBM and has taught at Brigham Young University, the University of Michigan, the University of Kentucky, and Auburn University.

## CRITICAL RECEPTION

### *The Upside*

"What a profound and timely book! Here is the cure for arguments and misunderstandings; for mediocrity and frustration. This book offers a wealth of principles and skills that will dramatically improve your career, your organization, and your relationships," writes Stephen R. Covey, author of *The 7 Habits of Highly Effective People*. Ivana Taylor, writing for *Small Business Trends*, proclaims the professional benefits of the book: "Business owners will benefit by upgrading their conversations in a way that will eliminate fear and intimidation among their teams. ...Sales and marketing professionals will learn how to put customers at ease and negotiate more profitable deals."

Many reviewers enjoy the format and style of *Crucial Conversations*, praising it for its simplicity and usability. Carolyn Rogers, a writer for EDWorks's *Expect Success* blog, finds the opportunities for self-reflection embedded within the text useful for processing the skills introduced. She also appreciates the video links provided by the authors in this second edition, which further illustrate the book's principles. Jill Jensen of the

Jensen Group finds it easy to relate to the real-life examples highlighted throughout the chapters and remarks on the authors' great sense of humor. She also notes how helpful the many acronyms are for remembering the steps to take in high-stakes situations.

Other reviewers laud specific concepts within the book for their insight and clarity. Cherie Burbach, writing for About.com, finds the concept of contrasting extremely helpful, and praises the wisdom of "owning your emotions" and not using other people as an excuse for how you feel. Nathan Albright of the *Edge Induced Cohesion* blog remarks on the book's sage advice on preserving safety and maintaining awareness of threats to meaningful and polite conversations. He also found it useful for identifying failures in his own conversational style: "Reading this book, I saw a great deal of bad conversation habits I have that turn many crucial conversations into ugly verbal battles."

Dain M. Hancock, president of Lockheed Martin Aeronautics, sings the book's praises: "Most books make promises. This one delivers. These skills have not only helped us to change the culture of our company, but have also generated new techniques for working together in ways that enabled us to win the largest contract in our industry's history."

## *The Downside*

Many reviewers thing that the book was simply too long. Fiona of the *Life Strategies* blog writes, "The authors did a very good job of getting the point across in the first few chapters, however after that the advice seemed a bit repetitive." And Jonathan Hoguet, writing on his blog, says: "It is disappointing to finish reading a paragraph or page and then say—wow—that didn't really add anything new."

Others have difficulties with the book's content. Cherie Burbach, on About.com, feels that the advice is too black and white and does not take special circumstances into account, arguing that some conversations require more time and deeper delving to uncover commonalities. Sharon at Goodreads feels that while the content is powerful, it will be challenging to use the tools effectively without opportunities for hands-on practice before an actual crucial conversation arises. And Mark Lamendola at Mindconnection.com questions the research, pointing out that the authors provide neither a bibliography nor references. He writes, "There is one page of end notes for the whole book."

Finally, Matt Moody, of CallDrMatt.com, finds issue with the book's lack of attention to process, feeling that it does not explain how to work through the more emotional components. He argues that telling readers not to have certain emotions is not enough. He also finds the idea of taking charge of the body overly simplistic, comparing it to telling green tomatoes to "be ripe." "The book creates the illusion that YOU CAN TAKE CONTROL of your stories and your emotions; this is an illusion because human beings cannot really CONTROL their stories or their emotions, especially in the moment when stakes are high. ..." Moody concludes, "[T]he book asks you to do many things, that you can't really do, unless you are an unflappable person of low emotion."

## SYNOPSIS

In eleven chapters, *Crucial Conversations* describes the paths that lead to self-destructive and explosive conversations, provides insight and practices for avoiding them, and illuminates the warning signs that a conversation may devolve.

In chapter 1 the authors describe what a crucial conversation is, explaining that the more important the conversation, the harder it is to master it. It's important to face difficult conversations head-on and with poise, rather than give in to the typical human tendency toward "fight or flight." If this skill is successfully learned, jobs, relationships, and personal health will all benefit.

Chapter 2 discusses the importance of dialogue and developing a pool of shared meaning in which people feel encouraged and safe to contribute their opinions and ideas. The key, the authors say, is to avoid silence and violence, the two most common destroyers of productive conversation.

In chapter 3 the authors stress the importance of "starting with heart," by paying attention to personal reactions in emotionally charged conversations, and making sure that unhealthy defenses are not employed. It's important to identify the goal desired from the conversation and to stay true to that purpose.

In chapter 4 the authors teach the art of viewing conversations through a broader lens: to look both at the content of discussions and at the conditions, paying particular attention to verbal and physical cues that may make others feel threatened. How is the conversation being handled? Is the greater purpose at the center of the discussion, or is it being strayed from?

Chapter 5 features strategies for maintaining safety throughout the entire conversation. One must make sure that the person on the other side of the conversation believes one's motives, and must also trust that he or she is being shown respect. If someone feels betrayed, apologize. The authors also provide helpful ways to return to a mutual purpose when communication has begun to deteriorate.

In chapter 6 the authors teach the art of mastering stories by avoiding emotionally driven scenarios and sticking to the facts. By neutrally identifying what has actually and factually occurred—rather than leaping to thoughts of what might have occurred—it becomes easier to consider other points of view and respond rationally.

The concept taught in chapter 7 is "STATE My Path": Sharing your facts, Telling your story, Asking for others' paths, Talking tentatively, and Encouraging testing. When this skill is successfully learned, it will be far easier to maintain dialogue, stay connected, and have a productive conversation.

Chapter 8 teaches the skill of exploring others' paths by expressing curiosity and exhibiting patience. When people are reluctant to share their views, encourage them by mirroring them and acknowledging what they appear to be feeling, paraphrase what you hear them saying, or, if all else fails, prime them by guessing what they are experiencing.

Finally, in chapter 9 the authors teach how to move to action by making decisions that follow through. It is critical to discern the approach to pursue: commanding, consulting, voting, or reaching consensus. Once a decision has been made, clearly determine who does what and when.

The authors include chapters 10 and 11 to address particularly challenging cases, providing a useful chart to follow in navigating crucial conversations. They give specific advice on how to confront typical issues, from insubordination to teenage excuses, and provide helpful insight into what to avoid along with how to proceed.

# Key Concepts of
# *Crucial Conversations*

All meaningful communication begins with **healthy dialogue**. The key to establishing and maintaining these conversations is **creating mutual purpose**, so that all parties are working toward a shared goal. Once all involved feel safe and respected, they are able to engage in **crucial conversations** about high-stakes topics and potentially emotional issues that lead to positive outcomes.

## I. HEALTHY DIALOGUE

Those who are skilled at having emotional and risky conversations are able to gather all the pertinent details. By encouraging open and honest sharing of opinions, feelings, and ideas, they create meaningful dialogue. To encourage this free flow of ideas, the authors advise to start with heart.

Starting with heart means looking inward to identify patterns of behavior during crucial conversations and to determine how to improve communication skills. The first step is recognizing that people can truly change only themselves. Rather than blaming others for their problems, identify the ways you are contributing and work to make a change. Begin by asking three questions: What do I want for myself? What do I want for others? What do I want for the relationship? Asking these questions helps clarify your motivations and directs you toward dialogue.

Unfortunately, when people are faced with stressful situations or feel pressure to perform or respond a certain way, they often revert to behaviors that can impede successful conversations. Sometimes they become overly focused on winning and lose sight of their original goals. At other times they may even become so angry that they feel a strong desire to hurt the other person. Both of these options break down healthy dialogue. A third option is to ignore the issue in an attempt to keep the peace. Returning to the three questions posed earlier as well as a new one—"How would I behave if I really wanted these results?"—forces you to pause and examine your behavior.

Sometimes when faced with emotional conversations, people become defensive and feel their options narrow to two choices: speak up at the risk of destroying the relationship or stay quiet but unhappy and maintain it. This is what the authors call the "Fool's Choice," and they suggest expanding the question to "What do I want for myself, the other person, and the relationship?" This more complex question is a reminder that there are many options—just be creative in finding them. The first step is clarifying what is really wanted; the second is to clarify what is not wanted. The "don't" helps frame what is desired for the relationship by identifying the fears that are driving their current negative actions. What might happen if those behaviors were abandoned? Posing a more complex question has the added benefit of reengaging the brain. When people are actively thinking, the body sends blood to the brain and away from the parts of the body that react with a fight-or-flight response.

Most crucial conversations fail because people do not pay attention to all the cues. They may notice that the person they are talking to is raising their voice or using stronger language, but they need to train themselves to look for nonverbal cues as well. They must be able to identify when others do not feel safe. As people become fearful, they tend either to withdraw into silence or to attack. Neither of these approaches leads to meaningful communication. As they view people exhibiting these behaviors, it is up to the skilled conversationalist to actively change the dynamic.

This process can begin by evaluating one's own style under stress, and the impact those actions have on others' feelings of safety. To evaluate your style under stress, you must be able to observe your own behavior in the midst of a crucial conversation. Pay particular attention to the tactics you revert to when you feel threatened. Do you mask your true opinions with sarcasm or sugarcoating? Do you completely avoid sensitive topics? Do you withdraw from a conversation when it starts to get tough? Do you try to control others by forcing your views on them? Do you label people or their ideas with stereotypes so that you can dismiss them? Do you attack or belittle? It is critical to understand how you may be negatively affecting a conversation in order to make the necessary changes that will lead back to healthy dialogue. Fortunately, the authors have many strategies for doing so.

According to the authors, facts are an important resource when trying to reestablish dialogue. Often, people become so enmeshed in what they are feeling or what they think others' motivations are that they fail to understand what is really going on. By focusing on facts, and asking yourself, "Can I hear or see this thing that I'm calling a fact?" imagined intentions can be separated from actual behaviors. Because facts simply describe what happened, facts are not controversial. For this same reason, facts can be very persuasive; it's hard to deny something that definitively happened. When discussions become heated, returning to the facts and starting fresh from what both parties agree to be true can reopen the flow of information. This also forces the brain into action; as the mind evaluates and analyzes what occurred, energy is drawn away from the emotions.

According to the authors, there are three tiers of dialogue. Those who are the least effective at dialogue do not understand how their tone, body language, and behaviors affect those around them. They also assume that there is only one right way: theirs. They will resort to whatever tactics they feel will help them win, often making everyone involved feel unsafe and defensive in the process. Those who are good at dialogue understand that being able to control their emotions is an important step toward meaningful discussion. They do their best to tamp down any emotions as they arise, but eventually they reach a point where they can no longer contain their feelings. In most cases this results in sarcasm, an explosion of angry words, or complete silence. Those who have mastered dialogue know how to act on their emotions by thinking through them. They investigate the issues that caused the emotion and trace their path of action back to its source, so that they can address the central issue. They also work hard to establish a mutual purpose.

## *Examples from* Crucial Conversations

- On the night before Bobbie B.'s first deployment to Iraq, he took part in a crucial conversation that ended quite badly. His family was dragged into the drama, and the damage from the fallout affected everyone: his siblings, cousins, aunts, uncles, parents, children, and grandparents. The effects of the conversation lingered, and each family reunion seemed to pull people farther apart. By the time he ended his tour in Baghdad, his family seemed irreparably broken. His silence with his father had lasted more than five years and prevented his two children from meeting their grandfather. Then, before his third tour of duty, he was invited to a Crucial Conversations training session led by a neighbor. That class changed Bobbie's life. A few weeks before he deployed, he reached out to his estranged father and spent three intense hours discussing their built-up pain and resentment. As he worked hard to create safe conditions filled with honesty and compassion, the truth emerged. When his emotions threatened to disrupt the meaningful dialogue, Bobbie focused back on their mutual purpose—rebuilding family relationships. After their talk, they joined Bobbie's mother and engaged in another crucial conversation. Today, Bobbie maintains loving relationships with his wife, parents, and children. He feels certain that without the strategies he learned in the Crucial Conversations training, his relationship with his father would never have been rekindled.

- In one study, a group of patients with malignant melanoma received traditional treatment before being separated into two groups. The first group met weekly for six weeks; the other group did not meet at all. The members of the first group were taught specific communication skills. Even though they had met only six times, the group of patients who had learned communication skills had a significantly higher survival rate than the other group after a five-year period. Only 9 percent of the trained group died from their disease, while almost 30 percent of the other group passed away.

- Lori A. has a daughter with bipolar disorder. For many years Lori and her husband watched their daughter abuse substances and cut herself, and had the police come to the house during violent episodes. After learning about crucial conversations, Lori began employing the STATE My Path skills in her dealings with her daughter. By removing judgment, sharing her concerns, and stating the facts, Lori was able to create an environment where her daughter felt comfortable sharing her own story, and was also able to hear her mother's words. Crucial conversations helped Lori maintain a relationship with her daughter during a time when emotions and resorting to silence or violence could have easily caused permanent damage.

## *Applying the Concept*

- **Practice learning to look.** It takes practice to learn to identify signs that the content or conditions of a conversation have made others feel unsafe. Become a keen observer of those around you: partners, kids, colleagues, neighbors, and teachers. Notice when their behaviors or tones shift and when they begin to withdraw or retreat into labeling or threatening. Make a mental note of what you think should be done to return the person to a feeling of safety.

- **Don't be a fool.** Most of us frequently fall prey to the trap of the Fool's Choice, the feeling that there are only two options and that neither of them will produce the outcome we desire. Purposefully set up low-stress situations where multiple opinions contribute to a decision, like choosing a family movie to watch or helping neighborhood kids create rules for a new game. Force yourself to contribute a solution in each scenario where everyone's needs are met, which serves the dual purpose of both practicing this skill and being a model for others.

- **Flex your brainpower.** Studies show that when people engage their brains it takes power away from reactionary or emotion-driven responses. When you feel yourself begin to become emotional, practice switching gears by presenting your brain with a complex problem. It can be as simple as remembering all the things you've had to eat for the past week or as challenging as a difficult math problem. Notice the shift in your body and your mood as you begin to work at the problem.

## II. CREATING MUTUAL PURPOSE

Healthy dialogue rarely occurs when mutual purpose has not been established. Creating mutual purpose ensures that everyone cares about the outcome and is invested in finding the best solution. It encourages every voice to be heard and guarantees that every opinion is valued and respected.

The authors call personal feelings, emotions, and experiences "pools of meaning." Each person brings their own pool of meaning to every interaction they have. Those who are able to build healthy dialogues work to create a shared pool of meaning that includes everyone's thoughts and input. The shared pool does not require unanimous agreement on the issues being discussed. Instead, it recognizes that each person has something valuable to contribute. As the shared pool gets larger, more information and ideas are shared, prompting better and smarter choices. When people contribute to a shared pool and feel heard, they are more likely to commit to the group's decision. The real danger occurs when people do not feel engaged with the process and dialogue ceases. In order to avoid this situation, the authors recommend establishing a mutual purpose.

Mutual purpose creates a shared goal and a positive environment for discussion. When mutual purpose is established, all parties believe that they are committed to the same outcome and that their goals, interests, and opinions are valued. When mutual purpose does not exist, conversations become debates and people resort to accusations and defensiveness. When this happens, the authors suggest trying to see the other person's point of view. When people understand others' motives, they can appeal to those desires and draw them into conversations they might otherwise avoid.

The partner to mutual purpose is mutual respect; both are essential to crucial conversations. When others don't believe their ideas and feelings are respected, they are unlikely to contribute to the conversation and likely to respond in fear or anger.

Sometimes people enter a crucial conversation with clearly different purposes, and bridging that gap to find a mutual purpose can be a challenge. The authors recommend applying four skills, which they collectively call CRIB: Commit, Recognize, Invent, and Brainstorm. By starting with heart, people need to agree to disagree while remaining in the conversation long enough to forge a solution that meets both parties' purposes. Doing so requires committing to not arguing and to being open to the possibility that there is a third choice that can satisfy both interests. By verbalizing the commitment to stay engaged in dialogue until a solution is reached, it is possible to create a safe environment for discussion. Once people have committed to working through a problem, they must be willing to try new approaches. Clearly stating each party's purpose will help people recognize what is truly at stake and open the door to new ideas.

Once each person's purpose has been clarified, it is time to be inventive. The goal is to create a mutual purpose that encompasses everyone's desires. Alternately people can work to identify a goal that is more meaningful or rewarding than each individual's original goals by looking to higher and longer-term objectives. Finally, once a shared purpose has been identified, dialogue can recommence, ideally to brainstorm strategies that feel mutually beneficial to all. This may require thinking outside the box and suspending judgment; when done successfully, creative solutions can unleash undreamed-of possibilities.

Successful crucial conversations can occur only when people feel valued and safe. When those two components are missing, communication breaks down, often with catastrophic results. People who don't feel safe in a conversation resort to one of two strategies: silence or violence. Those who are silent don't contribute to the shared pool, and those who are violent try to force their meaning above others'. People who hide in silence typically mask, avoid, or withdraw. When they mask, they either understate their views or show only pieces of their true feelings. Sarcasm, sugarcoating, and couching are all common displays of masking behavior. Those who avoid through silence stay far away from difficult topics, by either diverting or distracting with unrelated issues. Similarly, those who withdraw refuse to engage at all in the crucial conversation, often physically removing themselves from the discussion. On the other hand, those who turn to violence employ verbal attacks to force others toward their point of view. They control by dominating the conversation, label with stereotypes that they can easily dismiss, and threaten or belittle, all in an attempt to avoid a crucial conversation.

According to the authors, the best way to eliminate the risk of silence or violence is to be on constant lookout for safety violations. Doing so requires paying attention both to the content of the conversation and the conditions. It's much easier to spot when the content of a conversation has moved from open to unsafe: voices rise and the topic shifts or takes on a noninclusive tone. Noticing when conditions shift is trickier. Physically, people might notice tightness in their stomach or dry eyes; emotionally, they might feel afraid or angry. Behaviorally, they might raise their voice, point fingers, or retreat into silence. All these signs signal that the brain is disengaging and emotions are taking control. Noticing when others display these symptoms is critical to keeping conversations safe and productive. To restore safety in certain situations, it may be wisest to step away from the conversation. Once safety has been reestablished, conversation can begin anew.

Often, people feel unsafe in crucial conversations because of stories that can rise around an issue. While some stories are accurate and promote healthy results, more often than not stories are used to rationalize bad behavior. The authors urge people to pay particular attention to what they call "clever stories." There are three types of clever stories: victim stories, villain stories, and helpless stories. In victim stories, people are innocent, suffering from the bad choices or actions of others. Victims believe they have played no part in creating the problem and avoid any responsibility for their current situation. Villain stories are used to make others out as monsters; they exaggerate the slighted person's innocence as well as the blamed person's fault. When people employ villain stories, they often feel justified in further maligning the villains. Both victim and villain stories are merely caricatures of what has occurred and do not present the truth. Finally, helpless stories allow people to completely avoid a situation or conversation because they insist that they are powerless to create change. Because there is no healthy or helpful alternative, helplessness lends itself to negative choices and stagnation.

According to the authors, people employ these clever stories for several reasons. Occasionally, but not commonly, the clever story is accurate. More frequently, a clever story gives someone an out, because they relinquish all responsibility through it. Sometimes, clever stories keep people from having to accept their mistakes by providing an alternate explanation. Almost all clever stories are fabricated after a person fails to do something that they should have done. Fortunately, there is an alternative to clever stories: mastering the story. While clever stories purposefully omit important details, mastered stories try to uncover missing ones. Instead of becoming a victim, people work to identify their role in creating a problem. Instead of vilifying others, they ask themselves why a rational person would act that way.

Instead of becoming helpless, they focus on what they want for themselves, others, and the relationship, and work hard to realize those goals.

## *Examples from* Crucial Conversations

- When Bob arrives home from work, he can tell that his wife, Carol, is upset and has been crying. Instead of looking for comfort from him, she greets him with an accusatory, "How could you?" Without talking to him or looking for alternate explanations for the facts, she has leapt into a victim story. Earlier in the day, when she was looking at their credit card statement, Carol noticed a charge for a cheap motel close to their home and immediately assumed that her husband was having an affair. As she fumed and let her emotions overwhelm her conversational skills, Bob racked his brain for a reason that she could be so upset with him. Fortunately, Carol decided to stay in dialogue with Bob long enough to confirm or dismiss her suspicions. Starting with heart, she explained that she was checking the bill and noticed the charge for the motel. Although Bob wanted to deal with it later, Carol convinced him that it was important to her, and together they called the motel to investigate the charge. It turned out that when they were dining at a Chinese restaurant earlier in the week, the owner, who also owned the motel, used an imprinting machine that represented both establishments. Rather than letting the evidence drive her emotions and damage their relationship, Carol used the skills they had learned from *Crucial Conversations* to communicate effectively, and in the process strengthened her relationship with her husband.

- Kevin, the other seven vice presidents from his company, and their bosses were deciding on a new location for their office. The options were wide open: downtown, across the state, even across the country. When Chris, the CEO, pitched his preference, it was incredibly unpopular and posed potential threats to the company. Yet whenever anyone attempted to share their concerns, Chris reacted defensively, pointing his finger and raising his voice. Soon the group retreated into silence and it looked like Chris was going to get his way. Then Kevin, a masterful communicator, spoke up. He very calmly and respectfully explained what he was observing, namely that Chris was using his powerful position to sidestep his own decision-making guidelines and move the company to his hometown. After listening to Kevin's factual analysis, Chris agreed that he was being overly forceful and graciously reopened the discussion.

- Daryl was in the end stages of crucial negotiations with a key partner to develop a venture capital–funded company in Europe. Before meeting to discuss impasses in the deal, he reread *Crucial Conversations* to ensure that he fostered meaningful dialogue. During the six-hour meeting, Daryl redirected the conversation several times by restoring safety as he explored the other side's point of view. Eventually the two parties emerged with a deal. At the last moment, it looked like everything was going to fall apart over one word in the seventeen-page agreement. Rather than reverting to negative behavior patterns, Daryl stepped back, explored everyone's views, and restored safety by establishing a mutual purpose—and the issue was easily resolved.

## Applying the Concept

- **Fact or crap?** In this fun game, players race against one another as they try to determine whether a given statement is true or false. Try testing your fact sense by listening to conversations throughout your day. As people make comments, determine whether they are based on fact or on stories they have created in an attempt to interpret the facts.

Pay particular attention to the conclusions that you draw when people make comments to or about you.

- **Share the pool.** It's easy to convince ourselves that what we think is right or that we know best. Try inviting others to share their feelings, opinions, and ideas on current decisions. Practice using language that makes them feel valued and respected and establishes a mutual purpose. Remind yourself that strategy is different from purpose, and remember to ask yourself, "What do I want for me, for others, and for the relationship?"

- **Learn to respect the enemy.** There are always a few people in our lives whose values lie on opposite sides of the spectrum from our own. While learning to respect these people is challenging, searching for ways that they are similar to you can help. Choose three people that you struggle to respect and identify at least one thing that you have in common with each. If you get stuck, remind yourself that we all experience weaknesses.

## III. CRUCIAL CONVERSATIONS

According to the authors, a crucial conversation is a discussion where stakes are high, opinions vary, and emotions run strong. In this highly charged environment, most people fail to achieve their desired outcomes; in fact, many people avoid these interactions entirely. Fortunately, there are many strategies to help everyone involved in the dialogue feel heard, valued, and satisfied with the outcome.

One way to avoid flares is to make sure that everyone's intentions are properly received and understood. The authors suggest using a contrasting statement to clarify any misinterpretations. A contrasting statement includes a "don't," which addresses concerns of respect or purpose, and a "do," which confirms respect and clarifies intent. Here's an example: "I don't want to suggest that this problem is yours. The truth is, I think it is ours. What I do want is to be able to talk so that we can understand each other better." The "don't," which is the more important piece of the statement, explains what is not intended through actions or words. When that is established, it is harder for people to create stories surrounding motivations, and they are more likely to feel safe. The "do" defines the purpose and is used to move the dialogue in a positive direction. The authors are clear that contrasting provides context and proportion and should not serve as an apology. It confirms what you do and don't believe and creates a safe environment.

Sometimes people's intentions get muddied in their own minds by their emotions or stories. When this happens, the authors stress the importance of understanding the path to action. A path to action retraces the steps that a person took to arrive at their conclusion or reaction. It answers these questions: "Why am I retreating into silence?" "Why am I trying to force my opinions on the group?"

When retracing paths, the authors suggest taking note of your behavior, identifying your emotions, analyzing your stories, and focusing on the facts. As you evaluate your behavior, ask yourself how someone else would view your actions. Understanding what you are feeling in conjunction with those behaviors will provide more insight into the root causes. You may ask yourself if you are telling an accurate story or falling prey to a clever one. Separating the facts from the story can be very helpful. By focusing on what you see and hear, you may reach far different conclusions than you did during your initial, reactionary interpretation. Once you have become skilled at tracing your paths to actions, you can help others to do the same.

The authors offer four incremental tools for helping others understand why they retreat into silence or violence: Ask, Mirror, Paraphrase, and Prime (AMPP). The first step is to ask someone what they are feeling and invite them to share their concerns or elaborate on their position. For some people, simply asking them to contribute to the pool is enough. Others who are more reluctant to open up might respond to mirroring. When people mirror, they describe how another looks or acts, paying particular attention to physical cues and body language. It is important to keep the tone calm and the message emotion-free to show respect and maintain safety. An example message might be: "You say you're okay, but by the tone of your voice, you seem upset." Once this is said, paraphrasing their words in your own helps create additional safety and shows a sincere desire to understand. The authors warn against pushing too hard if a person is reluctant to share; instead, they suggest backing off. Priming should be used in situations where people are still closed up but seem to want to share. When people prime, they guess at what the other person is thinking or feeling in the hope that doing so will initiate a discussion. Priming should be employed only when nothing else is working.

In some cases, once all parties have shared their paths, they will recognize that they still disagree and feel that creating mutual purpose is unlikely. The authors promise that even in these situations, there is still the possibility for healthy dialogue. Sometimes, although people continue to debate and argue, they are actually in accord on 90 percent of the issues. Choosing to focus on insignificant details is unproductive, especially when both parties agree on the central issue. At this point, they should accept that they are in agreement and move on. Rather than homing in on the minute differences, skilled communicators attempt to identify points of consensus and then build. They may say, "I agree with what you are saying. In addition, I noticed that..." This can be an effective way to maintain safety while reviewing areas that need more attention. When absolutely no agreement can be found, the authors recommend comparing paths. Using statements such as "I think I see things differently. Let me describe how. ..." is an excellent way to acknowledge differences without decreeing them wrong or bad. In some instances, comparing differences may lead to a greater understanding and appreciation for another's viewpoint.

Becoming skilled at crucial conversations is important, but this must be backed up with a solid plan for action and decisions. It is critical to establish clear expectations about how decisions will be made and who will work to enact those decisions. The authors stress that dialogue and decision making are distinctly different; one works best with everyone's input and the other can be most productive with fewer voices. Those in positions of authority—parents, teachers, managers—should be in charge of making decisions, using one of four methods: commanding, consulting, voting, or reaching consensus. A command decision is made without any involvement and may be presented as a demand from an outside source or a choice to let someone else take the lead. With consulting, people invite experts to weigh in, evaluate all the options, and finally decide on a course of action. Voting is a helpful strategy if efficiency is the goal. It is usually a quick process and is most successful when the people voting understand that they may not get their top choice. When time is not an issue, consensus is an excellent way to create unity and a strong mutual purpose. The authors caution that consensus can also waste tremendous amounts of time and should be used only when stakes are high, issues are complex, or unanimity is required.

When considering which decision-making technique to choose, people should ask themselves several questions. Who wants to be involved? Who are the experts? Whose cooperation is essential for success? How many people is it worth involving? When a final decision is made, it should include a specific person or group that will complete the assignment, a detailed description of each task, a distinct deadline, and a method of following up on the progress being made. Documentation is also critical. The authors recommend writing down all the pertinent details, conclusions, decisions, and assignments in order to consult this information at key points in the process and ensure that the results of all the hard work are realized in a timely fashion.

## *Examples from* Crucial Conversations

- Dr. Jerry was working with a patient who had been admitted for vascular bypass surgery to repair circulation in her leg. The patient lived in Memphis and had traveled two hours for the operation. The procedure went smoothly, and the case manager and physician agreed that if all was well, she could be discharged the following Thursday afternoon. On Thursday morning, the case manager called the woman's husband to come to pick her up, unaware that the surgeon had decided to discharge her on Friday morning. When the woman tried to contact the surgeon, he said that he was headed home and absolutely needed to see her before she was released, so it would have to wait until the morning. At this point, Dr. Jerry stepped in. He spoke with the surgeon and explained that the patient's husband had driven two hours to get her, but when the surgeon responded defensively, saying, "Is the insurance company putting you up to this? Why are you pressuring me?" Dr. Jerry used the contrasting skill he had learned from *Crucial Conversations* and explained that his request *did not* reflect the desires of the insurance company, and that he *did* want to ensure that the patient and her family ended their experience with the hospital as happily as it had begun, an outcome that he was afraid would be marred by being forced to wait another day to go home. His efforts paid off, and the surgeon agreed to come in that evening to discharge his patient.

- When decisions are made, it is essential to articulate exact deliverables. As an example, the authors retell the apocryphal story of Howard Hughes's steam-powered car. In 1925, Hughes assigned a team of engineers the task of building a vastly improved steam-powered car. At the time, contemporary steam cars, such as the Doble and Stanley Steamer, required water every 60 miles and many minutes of heating to produce the steam needed. Hughes explained that he wanted a vehicle that would get 400 miles on a fill and instantly steam up, but that was the extent of his directive. To solve the problem of getting steam instantly, allegedly the engineers ran dozens of radiator pipes through the prototype car's body and passenger compartment. Unfortunately, they had not taken safety into account. When Hughes asked the engineers what would happen if the car got into a wreck, he was met with silence. At the realization that high-pressure steam would burn the passengers to death, the project was permanently abandoned. While this version of the story is disputed, the tale as told by the authors certainly shows what could happen when precise deliverables are not clearly stated.

- In a study of more than seven thousand doctors and nurses, the authors found that 84 percent of caregivers regularly see doctors or people in positions of authority taking shortcuts, making bad decisions, or breaking the rules. In those scenarios, the odds of a nurse voicing his or her concerns are less than one in twelve. The odds of a doctor speaking up are not much better. When people don't know how to engage effectively in crucial conversations, patient safety, medical staff turnover, and overall quality of care can suffer greatly.

## *Applying the Concept*

- **Decisions, decisions.** Make a list of the important decisions you make. If they are decisions you make alone, create the list alone. If they are decisions you make with a partner or a team, create the list with those individuals. Then think about or discuss how each decision is *currently* made and how it *should* be made using the decision-making strategies from the book. Keep notes during the exercise to use in the future when real decisions need to be made.

- **Mirror, mirror, on the wall.** Sometimes the best way to let someone know that what they say is being heard and that their opinions are valid is through mirroring. Next time you find yourself in a disagreement, practice sharing with the other person what you are observing and the concerns you have associated with that behavior. Use words like "you seem" or "I'm sensing" to convey that you are trying to understand their perspective, not forcing your analysis upon them.

- **Agree to disagree.** Having a successful crucial conversation has nothing to do with establishing who's right and who's wrong. Next time you feel inclined to assert your certitude, try refraining instead. Respond to a person with strongly different viewpoints than your own with statements such as "I think I see things differently. Let me describe how." This will help to continue the dialogue and reach a respectful understanding of each other's positions.

## Key Takeaways

- Healthy dialogue is the key to any productive crucial conversation. By first looking inward and assessing their style under stress, people can identify how they react in high-stakes or emotional interactions, and subsequently take measures to eliminate any ineffective strategies. They can learn to manage their emotions by reengaging the brain with the following complex question: "What do I want for me, the other person, and for the relationship?" When all else fails, turn to the facts to help reestablish meaningful dialogue.

- When all parties involved are working toward a mutual purpose, crucial conversations are highly successful. Effective communicators invite all opinions and feelings to be shared in a mutual pool of meaning. Doing so creates a wealth of knowledge and information that can lead to exceptional outcomes. Good communicators also work to create a safe environment by keeping watch on both the content and conditions of the conversation. By understanding the negative power of stories, people can avoid victimizing, vilifying, and pleading helplessness. Instead, they can take an active role in working toward a solution.

- Effective crucial conversations require constant attention and effort. As people begin to feel unsafe, they should retrace their paths to action to identify the source of their feelings and propose alternate motivations. Contrasting statements can also be helpful in clarifying intent and reestablishing open dialogue. When others are reluctant to share, people can attempt to draw them out through AMPP: asking, mirroring, paraphrasing, and priming. When it's time to develop a plan of action and make decisions, it's essential to establish detailed tasks to be completed by specific people within a determined time frame.

---

# A Final Word

By definition, crucial conversations are tense, involve high stakes, and often arise around emotional issues. They are ripe with conflict and often devolve as people retreat into silence or violence. Fortunately, they can also be unifying, empowering, and highly successful.

Avoiding negative outcomes starts with understanding why people react the way they do, and knowing how to create a safe environment in which everyone feels comfortable contributing to the shared pool of meaning and engaged in working toward a mutual purpose. Creating healthy dialogue depends on both the ability to manage reactions in emotional situations and the ability to help others feel valued and respected. The first step toward a resolution is simply committing to resolving the issue. Once that commitment has been made, people can work to find a mutual purpose and can brainstorm solutions that satisfy the desires of all involved.

To do this, people must be able to break through the layers of emotions and stories to uncover what is true. Almost every heated interaction can be retraced from actions back to emotions back to a story back to facts. When the facts are revealed and the brain becomes engaged in the process, it is often possible to see things from another person's point of view.

Sometimes people cannot find a mutual purpose, and they must work even harder to identify points of agreement, find places to build, and compare positions so that they can at least reach a place of mutual understanding. In general, most people just want to feel that they are heard and that others value their contributions. The difference between a disastrous crucial conversation and a meaningful one depends on whether those conditions are realized.

You have now glimpsed into the authors' collaborative work on communication. Now that this review has broken down some of the complex ideas in *Crucial Conversations*, you will get even more out of reading the complete book.

# Key Terms

**contrasting statement**   a statement that defines what a person hopes to get from the conversation and what they wish to avoid. A contrasting statement is used to rebuild **safety** by assuring others that they are respected, and that the intent behind the conversation is to benefit all involved. It clarifies purpose, and by doing so, helps to soften others' emotions and dispel the false **stories** they may have built around the conversation. Different than an apology, a contrasting statement simply provides context and proportion.

**crucial conversation**   any conversation in which opinions vary, stakes are high, and emotions run strong. Crucial conversations can arise at any time; they can be planned well ahead, like a conversation with the boss to discuss a promotion, or they can pop up in the middle of a discussion with a teenage child about what they did at school that day. Crucial conversations differ from normal conversations because the outcomes can have a dramatic impact on the quality of a person's life. Handling crucial conversations successfully depends on avoiding the natural inclination for fight or flight and instead engaging calmly and respectfully in a safe and open discussion.

**dialogue**   the free flow of meaning between two or more people. Healthy dialogue can occur only when people feel safe to share. When people openly contribute their opinions, ideas, and feelings, even when they are unpopular, the pool of information becomes much richer and better outcomes result. According to the authors, dialogue skills are learnable; as people pay attention to conditions in themselves and others, they can effectively promote talking, listening, and acting together.

**facts**   what a person actually sees and hears. The surest way to recover from out-of-control emotions or a burst of negative behaviors is to identify the facts. Facts are not controversial and can provide a starting point for **dialogue**. While facts are interpretable, they are not insulting or threatening. When a person explains the facts that led to a conclusion, it helps others to understand their point of view and provides an opportunity for others to clarify their purpose or meaning. Examining facts also reengages the brain, moving blood away from the parts of the body that react with fight or flight.

**Fool's Choice**   the mistaken conclusion that there are only two viable options: speaking up and turning an ally into an enemy or suffering in **silence**. This belief is learned at a young age, in family relationships and on the playground, and follows people into their professional and personal lives. The way to avoid falling into the trap of the Fool's Choice is to expand the question to: "What do I want for myself, the other person, and the relationship?" When people refuse to make a Fool's Choice, they free themselves to come up with creative solutions that benefit everyone involved.

**mutual purpose**   helping others see that everyone is working toward a common outcome in a conversation and that each person's goals, interests, and values are important. According to the authors, mutual purpose is the first condition in establishing **safety**. When mutual purpose is threatened, people become defensive and begin to promote hidden agendas. To return to mutual purpose, people should ask themselves the following two questions: "Do others believe I care about their goals in this conversation?" and "Do they trust my motives?" When people feel that their views are understood and appreciated, they become more willing to engage in **crucial conversations**.

**path to action**   the process that people follow when they are engaged in **crucial conversations**. The path to action flows from **facts** that people see and hear to **stories** that they create to explain those facts to emotions that stem from the stories they've told to actions or behaviors that protect them from those feelings. The key to recovering from negative actions is to retrace the path to action until the facts are clear. When people identify the facts, they are able to form different stories that encourage effective discourse and successful outcomes.

**safety**   the crux of any **crucial conversation**. When safety is violated or people perceive this is so, the conversation falls apart. When safety is evident, people become willing to share their ideas, opinions, and feelings on almost any topic. Successful communicators learn to look for signs that safety is at risk and work hard to correct the issue. When safety has been severely threatened, people should step away from the central issue and focus all their energies on restoring safety; only then can meaningful conversation recommence.

**silence**   along with **violence**, one of the defense mechanisms that people resort to when faced with a **crucial conversation**. When people retreat into silence, they actively withhold information from the pool of meaning in an attempt to sidestep the discussion. Silence can take three forms: masking, avoiding, and withdrawing.

**stories**   something people tell themselves to add meaning to another's actions. People create stories between the moments that they observe another's behavior and when they feel an emotion related to that behavior. When people use stories to justify their bad decisions, they become victims or helpless players, and others are turned into villains. The trick is creating an accurate story that reflects what has actually occurred rather than a person's insecurities and fears. Learning to master their stories helps people control their emotions and improves the results of **crucial conversations**.

**violence** along with **silence**, the most common defense mechanism that people use when faced with **crucial conversations**. When people move to violence, they employ verbal strategies in an attempt to control the situation. Violence has three common forms: controlling, labeling, and attacking. Controlling occurs when people try to force others to accept their line of thinking by cutting them off, overstating their **facts**, or changing the subject. When people label, they apply a stereotype or gross generalization that allows them to quickly dismiss someone's thoughts and ideas. Attacking involves belittling or threatening others into promoting a point of view.

# Recommended Reading

In addition to *Crucial Conversations: Tools for Talking When Stakes Are High,* **second edition** (McGraw-Hill, 2011), the following books are recommended for anyone who wants to learn more about successful strategies for engaging in difficult yet effective conversations with their bosses, peers, and loved ones.

### Chalmers Brothers, *Language and the Pursuit of Happiness* (New Possibilities Press, 2004)

Certified personal coach Brothers explains the role that language and conversations play in influencing people's achievements. He promises that by approaching language as more than just grammar and words, people can use it to become more open and to redesign their personal and professional lives. With the direction provided by this book, language can free readers from unhealthy patterns, behaviors, and outcomes and help them build mutually beneficial relationships.

### Roger Fisher and Daniel Shapiro, *Beyond Reason: Using Emotions as You Negotiate* (Penguin, 2006)

Fisher, the director of the Harvard Negotiation Project, and Shapiro, a Harvard psychologist, team up to provide a guide on how to use emotions to shape the outcomes of disagreements. Readers learn to identify the five "core concerns" that underscore most emotional challenges, and how to use them to improve their relationships and achieve positive results.

**Roger Fisher, William Ury, and Bruce Patton, *Getting to Yes: Negotiating Agreement Without Giving In*, revised edition (Penguin, 2011)**

Originally published thirty years ago, *Getting to Yes* provides step-by-step strategies for all levels of conflict resolution and negotiation. Based on the work of the Harvard Negotiation Project, it teaches readers to reach mutually acceptable settlements in professional and personal arenas without becoming emotional or sacrificing values.

**Kerry Patterson, Joseph Grenny, Ron McMillan, and Al Switzler, *Crucial Confrontations: Tools for Resolving Broken Promises, Violated Expectations, and Bad Behavior* (McGraw-Hill, 2004)**

Based on twenty years of research and more than ten thousand hours of observation, this follow-up to *Crucial Conversations* provides strategies to resolve broken promises, violated expectation, and bad behavior in a way that actually strengthens relationships. From confronting a teenager about a new tattoo to addressing insubordination to telling an elder family member he or she is no longer safe to drive, *Crucial Confrontations* teaches readers to approach sensitive issues with confidence and grace.

**Susan Scott, *Fierce Conversations: Achieving Success at Work and in Life One Conversation at a Time* (Penguin, 2002)**

In this guide to powerful communication, Scott teaches readers to transform their conversations so that they deliver a more effective message. Using a step-by-step approach through her "Seven Principles of Fierce Conversations," she teaches how to overcome barriers to productive conversation, enrich personal and professional communications, improve clarity to boost understanding, and master strong emotions.

**Douglas Stone, Bruce Patton, and Sheila Heen,** *Difficult Conversations: How to Discuss What Matters Most,* **with a foreword by Roger Fisher, revised edition (Penguin, 2010)**

Rather than avoiding uncomfortable conversations, the authors provide tools for communicating with less stress toward more successful outcomes. Readers will learn to understand the scaffolding of difficult conversations, approach conversations with an open mind, listen for underlying motivation and meaning, stay calm, and effectively problem-solve.

**William Ury,** *Getting Past No: Negotiating in Difficult Situations,* **revised edition (Bantam, 1993)**

Based on his experiences at Harvard Law School's Program on Negotiating, Ury provides strategies for turning adversaries into allies. Readers will learn to stay calm in the face of stressful situations, defuse anger and hostility, understand others' intentions, and build creative outcomes that satisfy the desires of everyone involved.

**William Ury,** *The Power of a Positive No: Save the Deal Save the Relationship and Still Say No* **(Bantam, 2007)**

Ury provides a three-step method to delivering a "Positive No," one that does not destroy relationships or anger and alienate people. Readers will learn to assert and defend their interest, deliver a strong and firm no, and resist tricks and bullying from the other side, all while getting to a yes that satisfies their needs. Learning to effectively say no frees people to say yes to the things that truly matter.

# Bibliography

**Nathan Albright, "Book Review: *Crucial Conversations*"**
*Edge Induced Cohesion* (blog), July 11, 2011
http://edgeinducedcohesion.wordpress.com/2011/07/11/book-review
  -crucial-conversations

**"Al Switzler Biography"**
VitalSmarts, accessed May 15, 2013
http://www.alswitzler.com/pages/biography.html

**"Book Review—*Crucial Conversations*"**
Profitune Business, accessed May 24, 2013
http://www.profitune.com/Business-Improvement-Articles/Business-Management/
  book-review-crucial-conversations.htm

**Cherie Burbach, "*Crucial Conversations*"**
About.com, accessed May 24, 2013
http://friendship.about.com/od/Friendship-In-Culture/fr/
  Crucial-Conversations.htm

**"Company Leadership"**
VitalSmarts, accessed May 15, 2013
http://www.vitalsmarts.com/about-us/company-leadership

**"*Crucial Conversations: Tools for Talking When Stakes Are High*"**
iTunes Expanded Apps, last modified September 5, 2012
https://itunes.apple.com/us/app/crucial-conversations-tools/id455488328?mt=8

*"Crucial Conversations: Tools for Talking When Stakes Are High"*

VitalSmarts, accessed May 15, 2013

http://www.vitalsmarts.com/crucialconversations

**Fiona, "Book Review: *Crucial Conversations"***

*Life Strategies* (blog), September 8, 2009

http://career-engagement.blogspot.com/2009/09/book-review-crucial-
conversations.html

**Jonathan Hoguet, "[Book Review] *Crucial Conversations: Tools for Talking
When the Stakes Are High"***

*Jonathan Hoguet* (blog), January 7, 2012

http://jonhoguet.blogspot.com/2012/01/book-review-crucial-conversations-
tools.html

**Jill Jensen, *"Crucial Conversations: Tools for Talking When Stakes Are High"***

The Jensen Group, accessed May 24, 2013

http://showcase.netins.net/web/jjjensen/books/book26_CrucialConversations.html

**Joseph Grenny**

Personal website, accessed May 20, 2013

http://www.josephgrenny.com

**Mark Lamendola, "Book Review of: *Crucial Conversations"***

Mindconnection, accessed May 24, 2013

http://www.mindconnection.com/books/crucialconversations.htm

**Matt Moody, *"Crucial Conversation: Tools for Talking When Stakes Are High—
Idea Analysis"***

CallDrMatt.com, accessed May 24, 2013

http://www.calldrmatt.com/Crucial_Conversations_Tools_for_Talking.htm

**Carolyn Rogers, "Book Review of *Crucial Conversations*"**

EDWorks: *Expect Success* (blog), April 13, 2013

http://edworkspartners.org/expect-success/2013/04/book-review-of-
crucial-conversations

**Ron McMillan**

Personal website, accessed May 20, 2013

http://www.ronmcmillan.net

**"Sharon's Review: *Crucial Conversations: Tools for Talking When Stakes
Are High*"**

Goodreads, August 27, 2010

http://www.goodreads.com/review/show/113856640

**Ivana Taylor, "*Crucial Conversations: Tools for Talking When Stakes Are High*"**

*Small Business Trends*, October 22, 2011

http://smallbiztrends.com/2011/10/crucial-conversations-book-review.html

Lightning Source UK Ltd.
Milton Keynes UK
UKOW05f1811030913

216483UK00001B/22/P